Classic Instruction

Other books by The American Golfer

*The Hogan Mystique**

*Bobby Jones: The Greatest of Them All**

*Byron Nelson: The Story of Golf's Finest Gentleman
and The Greatest Winning Streak in History**

The 25 Greatest Achievements in Golf

The Players Championship: 25th Anniversary

The World Golf Hall of Fame

*Copublished with Broadway Books

Classic Instruction

by Bobby Jones and Ben Crenshaw

Edited by Martin Davis

THE AMERICAN GOLFER

Greenwich

BROADWAY BOOKS

New York

Photographs of Ben Crenshaw by Steve Szurlej.
Photograph on doublegate opener by ALLSPORT.

FIRST EDITION

ISBN 0-7679-0208-4

98 99 00 01 10 9 8 7 6 5 4 3 2 1

Copublished by:
The American Golfer, Inc.
151 Railroad Avenue
Greenwich, Connecticut 06830
(203) 862-9720
FAX (203) 862-9724

Broadway Books
1540 Broadway
New York, New York 10036
(212) 354-6500

Design by:
ALL CAPS
599 Riverside Avenue
Westport, Connecticut 06880
(203) 221-1609

Prepress by:
Graphic Productions
282 Main Street Extension
Middletown, Connecticut 06457
(860) 704-2220

For Charlie Yates, a great friend of golf and a great friend of Bob Jones.

"To me, his style of writing was as elegant as his own swing, and will always be an important part of golf's literature."

—BEN CRENSHAW
from *Bobby Jones: The Greatest of Them All*

Contents

Foreword 12

Introduction 14

⊰⊱⬦⊰⊱

The Grip 20

Woods 28

Long Irons 46

Short Irons 62

Sand Play 74

Putting 94

Chipping 120

The Stymie 140

⊰⊱⬦⊰⊱

Classic Instruction
by Martin Davis

While I was researching my earlier biography on Jones, *Bobby Jones: The Greatest of Them All*, I was given access to Bob's files and memorabilia at Alston & Bird, the law firm in Atlanta that Bob helped establish. In a conference room, aptly named after him and featuring the original architect's rendering of the Augusta National Golf Course, were assembled approximately 20 boxes of assorted records and photographs for my review. Many of the pictures in these boxes chronicled Bob's life and had never been published. The Jones family kindly gave me permission to use these in my biography of Bob.

As I pored through these boxes, I came across a small black box containing approximately 100 instructional photos of Bob Jones with numbers on the back keyed to a series of handwritten yellow legal pages covering each aspect of the game—the grip, woods, long irons, short irons, sand play, putting and chipping. Looking through the box, my eyes widened. It was as if I had discovered the Rosetta Stone for golfers—the keys to the game handwritten by the master himself!

Among true golf afficionados, I doubt there would be much debate with the notion that golf's popularity today is attributable, in large part, to what Bob Jones accomplished. Think, for a moment, about what he did.

Bob's record as a competitor is unparalleled: he won thirteen national championships in an eight-year span, with four of these—the British Amateur, the British Open, the U.S. Open and the U.S. Amateur—coming in the Grand Slam year of 1930. A lifelong amateur, Jones accomplished a feat no one has been able to duplicate to this very day. When Jones played against the leading professionals, the press referred to it as "Jones against the field." He was that good.

Bob also established a standard for golf as a game of personal honor and individual responsibility. He twice called penalties on himself in competition, probably costing him two additional national championships. When asked about it, he replied, "you might as well praise a man for not robbing a bank," his innate sense of modesty and decency shining through.

Bob founded the Augusta National Golf Club, was instrumental in the design of the course and began the Masters, the pinnacle of golf tournaments.

But beyond these grand accomplishments, he left us with much more. Bob Jones's ability to communicate — whether via the wonderful short Warner Brothers films he wrote and starred in or through his books and magazine articles — was as important as his exploits on the course. He gave us a sense of what the game was all about and how to play it.

Upon investigation, I learned that the materials I unearthed in that long forgotten little black box were used in a limited series of film strips sold in the mid 1930s. Incredibly, the manuscript and pictures had never been published. Needless to say, I asked permission to publish this treasure. To my great joy, Ben Crenshaw, an admirer of Bob Jones and a serious student of the game and its history, agreed to coauthor the book. To best illustrate Ben's commentary, Steve Szurlej, one of golf's finest instructional photographers, photographed Ben's actual swing, at approximately the same position and angle as was shown in the photos taken of Jones in 1933.

Interestingly, Ben had never met Bob Jones — Ben's first appearance at the Masters came shortly after Bob had passed away. However, given Ben's strong connection with Augusta and his feelings about Bob Jones's role in golf as well as the classic nature of Ben's golf swing, there can be no argument that there is a direct historical linkage between the two.

I hope you enjoy this unique collaboration.

INTRODUCTION

Classic Instruction

by Ben Crenshaw

To my way of thinking, Bob Jones was a true Renaissance man. He not only played the game of golf at its very highest level, but wrote about it as well as anyone ever has. Bob's instruction book, *Golf Is My Game*, along with Harvey Penick's insightful lessons, provided the basis for my learning the game.

As golfers, we are truly blessed with the wonderful body of literature that has developed around the game. No other sport I know boasts the high calibre of writers that golf has consistently produced through the years: Bernard Darwin, Herbert Warren Wind, Henry Longhurst, Pat Ward-Thomas, Grantland Rice, Dan Jenkins, Peter Dobreiner and Charlie Price, to name a few.

Bob Jones, perhaps the greatest of golf's champions, certainly belongs in this exalted company of fine writers. His books, *Down the Fairway*, *Golf Is My Game* and *Bobby Jones on Golf*, as well as his articles appearing in *The American Golfer* magazine, have had great impact on people's enjoyment and understanding of the game. Bob's unique ability to clearly and concisely convey his thoughts on the game in general, and on the swing in particular, is one of golf's greatest treasures.

The photographs and accompanying copy that Martin Davis unearthed in researching our earlier book on Jones were an unbelievable find. Given the quality of these materials, we have chosen to use Bob Jones's exact words as he wrote them in longhand in 1933, along with the very photos he selected to illustrate each element of the golf swing.

Virtually all of what Bob Jones wrote about in these pages is applicable today. As a supplement to what Bob wrote, I have attempted to emphasize certain points he is making and also to point out the differences in the way I approach the game.

Several recurrent themes throughout the book are worth mentioning.

First and foremost, Bob emphasized the importance of a proper grip. He felt a sound grip was the foundation for playing the game properly. I wholeheartedly agree.

Another theme is the narrow stance Bob

used throughout *all* of his shots. To illustrate this, we have superimposed on the photos of both Bob and myself at the address position with various clubs white guidelines indicating the width of our relative stances. In comparison with the way I stand to the ball, you will notice just how narrow Bob's address position was with all of his clubs, including the putter. Bob felt the narrow stance encouraged a proper turn back and through the ball.

This narrow stance provided him with the base to truly *swing* the club, another recurrent theme in the book. No other great golfer stood with such a narrow stance as Bob Jones.

As you can well imagine, because of the improvements in the implements we play with today and the strides made in course conditioning, the nature of the golf swing has changed somewhat from Bob Jones's day. Although Bob's swing was more of a "hands swing"— to compensate for the inherent torque of the hickory shafts, the basic fundamentals of proper form remain unchanged. It seems altogether fitting to hold this classic golf swing as a model for today's golfers.

As is widely known, Bob Jones had a very inventive and active mind.

He learned the game as a boy by copying his Scottish pro, Stuart Maiden, and experimenting with different techniques that seemed to work best for him. Luckily for us, these techniques also work well for most golfers

and continue to do so to this very day.

Today, it seems, the emphasis in the game is on power and hitting the ball high. It's a more violent game. To my way of thinking, Bob Jones's golf swing was far more elegant than many we see today. It was one of the most lyrical and rhythmical swings ever. It's just as Bernard Darwin said, "...there was a touch of poetry to it."

I urge you to try some of the techniques Bob and I describe on the following pages. I think it they will improve your game. At the very least, they should enhance your understanding of what goes into a good golf swing.

I have been truly fortunate to have won Bob's own tournament, the Masters, on two separate occasions. To now have the privilege of coauthoring a book with someone I so greatly respect, yet never met, is truly an honor.

I hope you enjoy the fruits of our labor — even though they occurred many, many years apart.

The Grip

Bob Jones believed that the foundation for a good golf swing was a fundamentally sound grip which enabled the left arm to play a dominant role in guiding the swing.

The grip I use does not differ much at all from Bob's grip.

JONES:

The first, and perhaps most important step towards learning golf is to acquire a correct grip. The hands must be placed upon the club in proper relation to each other, the face of the club and to other parts of the player's body.

The left hand must be placed in a position of power, to some extent on the top of the shaft. As I grip the club, I can see three knuckles of this hand as I look down upon it.

In order to make full use of the left arm, Jones employed a "strong" grip— he placed the left hand well over the shaft so that the left thumb was on the right side of the shaft and the first three knuckles of the left hand faced the golfer.

A few people these days advocate a little weaker grip in the left hand, but Jones' grip is still fundamentally sound. For example, Ben Hogan wanted his thumb on top of the shaft whereas Byron Nelson, Sam Snead and Jones definitely preferred a stronger grip.

As kids, Harvey Penick encouraged us to "…show him some left hand"— meaning using a strong grip as Bob Jones is doing here. It is a *very* powerful position.

JONES:

The right hand approaches the shaft in this way, with palm to the front, and grips the shaft in the fingers.

CRENSHAW:

It is important to note the way Bob is going to place his right hand on the club—with the web of his right hand and grasping the grip in the base of his fingers.

Harvey Penick taught me to grip the club in a similar way. He said grip the club like you would a yardstick.

Start with the web of your right hand to the side of the shaft and place the bottom of the shaft at the base of your fingers. Then simply wrap your fingers around it.

Harvey put it another way, "…simply shake hands with the club."

■ The Grip

CRENSHAW:

This is an excellent view showing the index finger separated from the other three fingers of the right hand. The thumb and the forefinger of the right hand provide feel and balance throughout the swing.

In terms of grip pressure, nothing much has changed today. Bob wanted to grip a little more firmly with his left hand and a little more sensitively with his right so that he could exercise control throughout the swing with his dominant left arm.

Proper grip pressure has the effect of unlocking the wrists.

JONES:

The grip must be positive, but never tense. The firmest pressure is exerted by the three smaller fingers (those visible here) of the left hand. The grip of the right hand is very light.

CRENSHAW:

I've always felt that if you grip the club too tightly, you won't be able to feel the clubhead.

I like to grip the club lightly enough so as to make the clubhead feel heavy when I swing. A smooth, rhythmical swing is not possible without feeling the clubhead.

Obviously, the converse is true: the tighter you grip it, the lighter the clubhead will feel, thereby lessening your ability to make a smooth swing.

Given today's equipment and the emphasis on power, we tend to grip the club a little tighter than in Bob Jones's day. However, sensitively gripping the club is still paramount.

JONES:

The little finger of
the right hand aids
compactness by
overlapping the index
finger of the
left, but...

CRENSHAW:

It is interesting to
note that Bob let his
right little finger rest
in the groove formed
between the index
and second finger of
his left hand. While
there are many
variations of the basic
grip, some better
players put the little
finger of the right
hand on top of the
second knuckle of the
index finger of the
left hand.

Whichever way you
grip the club, the
most important thing
is to position the two
hands and fingers so
as to achieve a secure
grip that works as
one piece.

…the fingers twine around the shaft providing an ample spread to make manipulation of the clubhead easy.

CRENSHAW:

Once again, proper grip pressure cannot be overemphasized in allowing the clubhead to swing.

To me, this photograph of Bob epitomizes proper grip pressure — it appears sensitive, ready and responsive. There is not a hint of tightness whatsoever.

■ Woods

JONES:

The first position should be comfortable. The feet are separated by approximately the width of the shoulders and both toes are turned slightly outward.

CRENSHAW:

I don't see how anyone could be more relaxed or better balanced over the golf ball. It's just the most beautiful position!

In viewing Bob's address position—a relatively narrow stance with his feet shoulder-width apart—remember that Jones was trying to put the club in motion by making full use of his hips and legs to achieve a full swing.

Bob always felt that the proper ball position with the driver was off the left instep so that there would not be any weight shift necessary to provide a sweeping motion through impact.

As you can see, I tend to stand a little wider than Bob. Today most people are taught to restrict their hip turn to 45° while fully turning their shoulders to 90°. To do so you should employ a wider stance.

Both approaches are valid. If you want to make full use of your body throughout the swing, use a narrower stance. If a more restrictive swing is desired, then stand a bit wider. Try both and see which makes more sense for you.

■ **Woods**

CRENSHAW:

Note how his arms hang down naturally and how it appears that he's ready to move in any direction. With a rounded back and straight legs, this is an "arms hanging" method. Although it's an older method, it looks so beautifully relaxed and comfortable that no one could go wrong by copying this set-up position.

JONES:

The stance is squared, that is, with the feet about equal distance from the line of play.

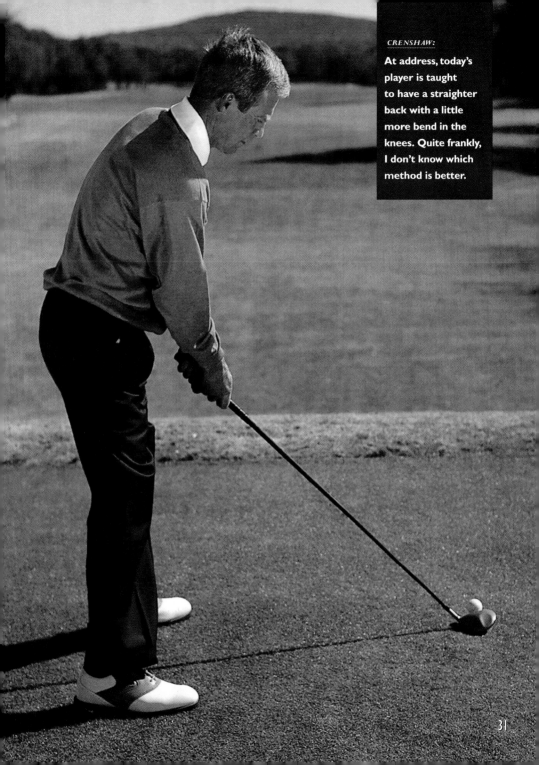

CRENSHAW:

Bob's takeaway definitely stems from the hickory-shafted era. His initial move away from the ball is quite similar to the one used by Byron Nelson—letting the clubhead drag its way back almost before the hips move. The hands move first and the feeling is that the clubhead is almost lagging behind.

Together with a narrow stance, the result is a full pivot and turn. If you feel that your body isn't turning, try this method.

JONES:

The backward movement originated in the center of the body. One has the feeling that the club is being pushed by the left side and left arm.

Today's takeaway employs a one-piece move away from the ball with the hands initiating the backswing. The hands, arms and shoulders move as one. Today, there are simply fewer independently moving parts.

I must say however that Bob's swing was more rhythmical and more lyrical than the ones we tend to see today.

■ Woods

CRENSHAW:

Today's golfer does not cock his wrists this early in the swing. This simply has to do with the takeaway itself.

Bob made ample use of his wrists, hands and arms in the backswing.

JONES:

The swing progresses for some distance before the hands begin to elevate the club and the first cocking of the wrists becomes apparent.

CRENSHAW:

Bob emphasized the importance of a full backswing. If that meant that the club went past parallel, that was perfectly fine.

He wanted a full hip and shoulder turn. He felt that the club was easier to keep in motion if there was a nice full turn.

Note how much his left heel comes off the ground—that's certainly one thing that's different from today.

In this position he is truly coiled.

JONES:

In completing the backward wind-up, the back is turned almost squarely to the hole. The swing is of ample length carrying the club past a horizontal position.

Today there is an emphasis on a shorter backswing with fewer moving parts so as to produce more of a "hit" at the ball.

Harvey Penick always taught that if you wanted a longer backswing, you should lift the left heel because it will add inches to your backswing.

31

■ Woods

CRENSHAW:

What an absolutely beautiful backswing! When Bob reached the top, he wanted the clubhead to cross the line and appear to be pointing to the right of his target. He felt that it was much easier to return your arms to your side, thus keeping your hands underneath the swing plane.

By swinging in this manner, you would not come over the top and produce a slice with a pronounced out-to-in swing path.

If you compare this photograph of Bob with the previous one, you'll note his hips are starting to unwind as he plants his left heel.

JONES:

The hips lead as the unwinding begins, and by pulling against the hands and the weight of the club, draw the left arm taut.

39

JONES:

The cock of the wrists is preserved during the early stages of the downstroke while the head of the club drops behind the player so that it can approach the ball from the inside.

CRENSHAW:

This is an ideal position. Significantly, there is no effort for the club to come out and over the intended line of flight. Putting the club in this position can only be achieved as a result of the proper unwinding of the left side during the early stages of the downswing. It cannot be achieved if the upper body takes over first.

Note carefully the position of the right elbow: it is close to the right side, but not cramped.

40

Every bit of power in the hips, legs and back
goes into the blow, which is directed along
the line upon which the ball
is intended to travel.

This is absolutely
perfect. Note how
Bob's left hip and left
side are out of the
way, making room for
the arms to come
through. His weight
has shifted to the
left side with his right
toe supporting his
right side; his right
knee, right hand
and right shoulder
are all kicking-in to
square the blow.

His head is still in
back of where the
ball was at address,
perfectly illustrating
the "stay-behind-the-
ball" school of
thought.

JONES:

The left arm remains perfectly straight and no roll of the right hand over the left takes place until after the ball has been started on its way.

CRENSHAW:

No one can achieve a more perfect position.

If you look at today's great players, you'll see that they all arrive at this same position regardless of how they start their swing. It is a very athletic position. Byron Nelson always said that a good position at impact is with the chin over the right knee.

There couldn't be a better image for golfers to keep in mind when they reach impact.

Note how Bob's left arm is ramrod straight. That's power!

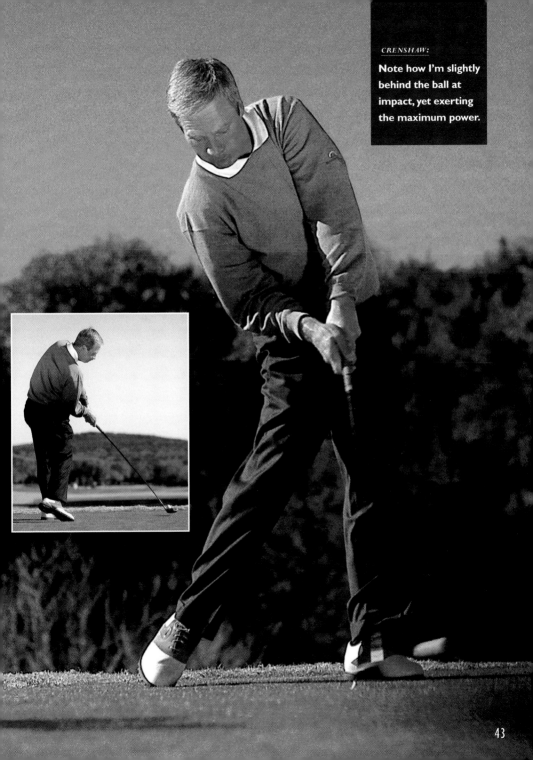

Note how I'm slightly behind the ball at impact, yet exerting the maximum power.

■ **Woods**

Again this is a great position to copy. What's important just past impact is how long Bob stays down and through the ball with his right shoulder coming under his chin. There's absolutely no effort to lift the ball into the air.

JONES:

A brassie shot from the fairway is hit hard and slightly downward in order to cause the ball to rise and pursue a controlled course.

44

45

■ *Long Irons*

JONES:

The spread of the feet here is greater than for the shorter clubs and smaller than when using the woods, but the position is otherwise the same.

CRENSHAW:

Note how Bob's feet are narrower than even his somewhat narrow stance with the driver.

The narrowness of the stance allowed Jones to swing the club further around his body. Remember that Jones' Scottish teacher, Stewart Maiden, learned to swing to keep the ball down and out of the wind. They played a "ground" or "running" game in the U.K.

As a result, the swing that Jones learned, especially with the longer clubs, was more around his body with a very full shoulder turn. He wanted a flatter swing that would produce a lower ball flight.

CRENSHAW:

Today's game is more of a power game or an "air" game with the objective to hit the ball high.

The stance at address is wider and the backswing is more upright.

Both approaches are certainly valid.

If you want to use more of your body in your swing, to unlock and activate your lower body, experiment with the width of the stance. You'll find more fluidity from the waist down with a narrower stance.

JONES:

The drag away from
the ball. The clubhead
lags because the
hips and legs start
the movement while
the hands and
wrists are relaxed.

CRENSHAW:

Bob's move away
from the ball is quite
different than the
way it is done today.
In the modern golf
swing, the clubhead
starts to move first.

CRENSHAW:

The backswing stays a little more on line and then it picks up, resulting in a higher hand position at the top of the swing.

49

■ **Long Irons**

JONES:

At this stage there has
scarcely been any change in
the relation of arms, hands
and club,…

CRENSHAW:

Notice how as **Bob**
is taking the club
back, his left foot is
already coming
off the ground early
in the backswing.

CRENSHAW:

In contrast, my left
foot tends to stay
on the ground for a
longer period of
time.

…but here the hands begin to pick up the movement as the turning of the hips and shoulders continues.

CRENSHAW:

As Jones turns away from the ball, note how he is markedly taking the club to the inside primarily with his hands.

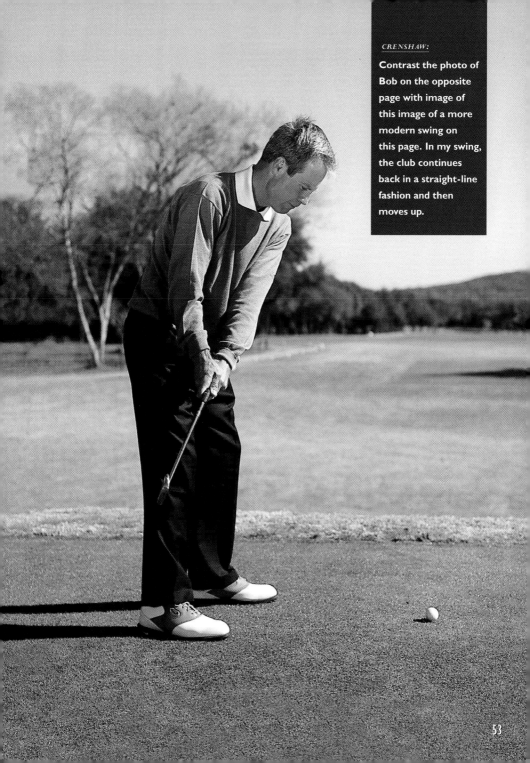

CRENSHAW:

Contrast the photo of Bob on the opposite page with image of this image of a more modern swing on this page. In my swing, the club continues back in a straight-line fashion and then moves up.

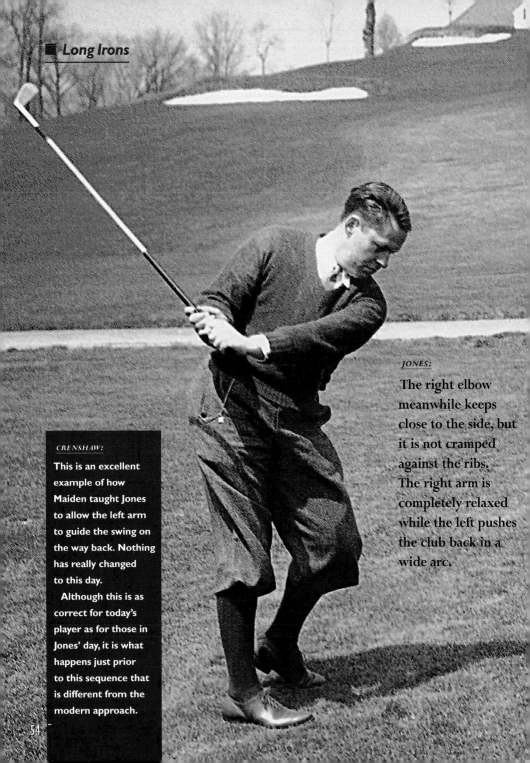

JONES:

The right elbow meanwhile keeps close to the side, but it is not cramped against the ribs. The right arm is completely relaxed while the left pushes the club back in a wide arc.

CRENSHAW:

This is an excellent example of how Maiden taught Jones to allow the left arm to guide the swing on the way back. Nothing has really changed to this day.

Although this is as correct for today's player as for those in Jones' day, it is what happens just prior to this sequence that is different from the modern approach.

JONES:

The wind-up of the hips is complete at this point. The club is about horizontal and the left arm shows a slight curve.

CRENSHAW:

Although this is a beautiful position at the top of the backswing, a player of today would most likely show less hip wind-up and have the left heel remain on the ground throughout the backswing.

JONES:

But here, an instant later, the hips have shifted a little towards the hole and begun to unwind while the club has continued moving up. The hands have been elevated and the wrist cocked completely, and the left arm has been pulled taut.

CRENSHAW:

Bob Jones wrote about the arms continuing to move back while the lower body begins to move downward. A difficult concept to grasp, I believe it was one of the peculiarities of Bob's swing.

While I don't think a modern-day instructor would teach this, I do believe Jones was simply mimicking what he saw in Stewart Maiden's swing.

A sound backswing completes the turn of the arms and shoulders and sets for just an instant before starting down. The most important thing to remember is that the left hip and left side initiate the downswing and the left foot gets firmly planted on the ground before the right half of the body begins to move.

JONES:

The hitting effort becomes, as shown here, a combination of the pull from the left side and the whipping action of the right forearm.

CRENSHAW:

This is simply the most perfect position one could study.

The hitting effort as shown here becomes a combination of a pull from the left side along with a whipping action of the right forearm.

This position is as true today as it was in Jones's day.

CRENSHAW:

In order to hit the ball solidly, the correct position of the club and arms is from the inside of the ball with the club going out to the target.

This is the total opposite position of the chronic slicer.

People slice because the upper body moves first before the lower body. When the upper body moves, the arms come out and "over" the top of the ball creating an outside-in swing path rather than more properly attacking the ball from the inside out to the target.

Every good player I have ever seen or studied gets in this very position. It's a key to good golf.

■ Long Irons

JONES:

The left leg, straightening suddenly at the knee just before contact, produces a thrust up the left side which greatly increases the power of the stroke. To hold the player down against this thrust is the duty of the head and right side of the body.

CRENSHAW:

You will see many players today who appear to have a little more bow in their left knee than what is depicted here. You'll note that Bob is using his hands more in this part of the swing than Hogan or Nelson would.

Yesterday players employed more of a "hands" swing, while today we tend to use the muscles of the back, shoulders, hips and trunk. The modern player is taught to use his hands less and his body more.

The stroke must carry through without quitting. Here you can get some conception of the effort that has been put into this iron shot of over two hundred yards.

CRENSHAW:

No one ever stayed down and through the ball better than Bob Jones.

■ *Short Irons*

JONES:

At address the feet are
quite close together
to permit easy
movement of the hips
for this little shot.

CRENSHAW:

Once again, Bob's
stance was very
narrow.

Even with a shorter
swing he still wanted
fluidity in his knees
and hips in order
to get the timing
of the stroke. Very
clearly he didn't
want his upper body
isolated just for
a short shot. He
always thought about
a swing and turn.

JONES:

…the hands and wrists begin to assist in lifting the club to the top of the swing.

CRENSHAW:

Bob's concept of swinging the clubhead was still very acute even in the shorter strokes. He always felt that in order to swing the club, a longer swing was necessary to get the full length of the backswing.

Note that the ball position at address is nearer the back foot than the front one. The ball is placed in this position because you want to make a very precise, crisp blow.

The thought of hitting a short iron is more of an up-and-down motion. So many people fail to swing the clubhead, especially with a short club.

The key to short iron shots lies in the set-up and how the weight is distributed. Although I use a somewhat wider stance than Bob, my weight is slightly biased to my left side.

■ Short Irons

JONES:

This is not a full swing, but it is about as far as I like to go with a lofted club for the sake of control.

CRENSHAW:

If you have a short, abbreviated stroke, the tendency is to try to hit the ball rather than swing through it. With a short swing, it becomes a stab or a lunge, with the extra effort trying to move the ball a certain distance.

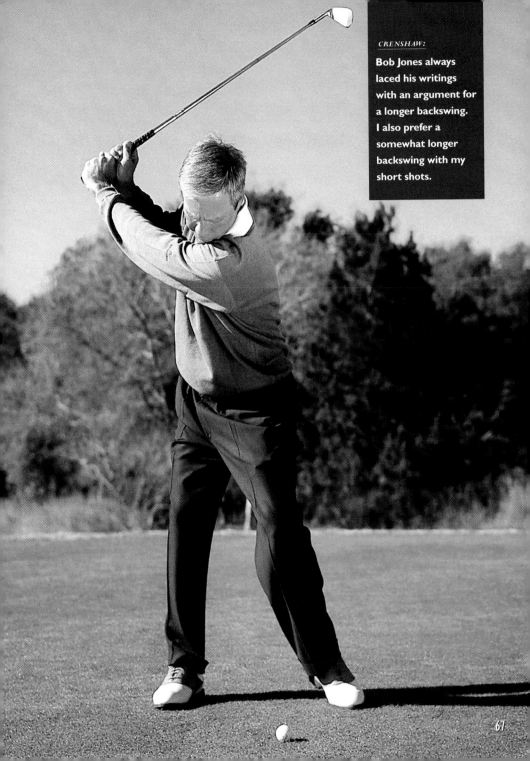

JONES:

The start down has been leisurely and the wrist-cock has been preserved almost intact.

CRENSHAW:

Bob Jones made a conscious effort to delay the wrist cock in the forward swing until the very last minute because his swing is a little steeper with a short iron.

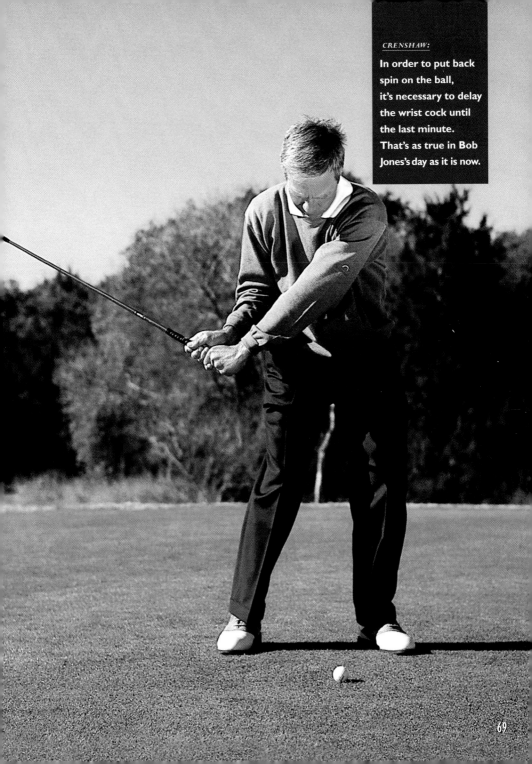

In order to put back
spin on the ball,
it's necessary to delay
the wrist cock until
the last minute.
That's as true in Bob
Jones's day as it is now.

JONES:

The stroke is directed slightly downward so that the club rips a divot from the turf after striking the ball.

CRENSHAW:

Again, any good player will try to arrive in this position. He must have the concept of pinching the ball against the turf.

Bob's concept of
the movement and
timing of a swing
is still very valuable
today.

If your short
game is made up
of short choppy
strokes, concentrate
on swinging the
weight of the club.

JONES:

The straight left arm,
the immovable head
and the action of
the right shoulder
and right arm hold
the player down
to the ball until it has
been started away.

■ Short Irons

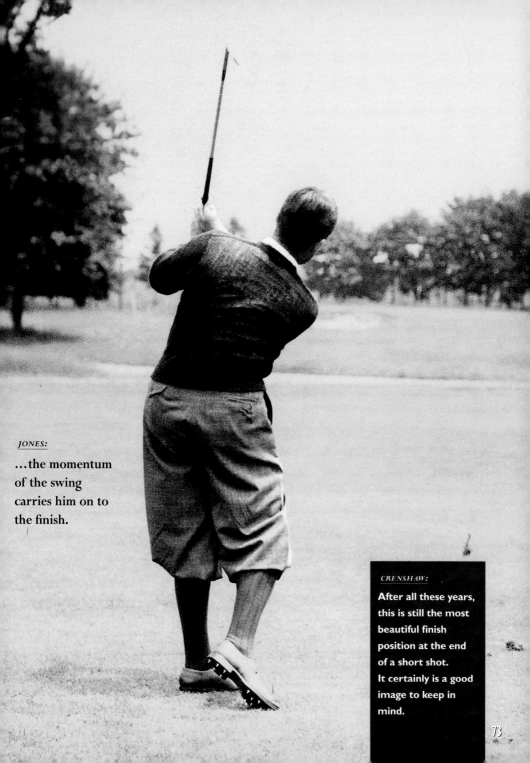

JONES:

...the momentum of the swing carries him on to the finish.

CRENSHAW:

After all these years, this is still the most beautiful finish position at the end of a short shot. It certainly is a good image to keep in mind.

73

■ Sand Play

In playing a full blast or explosive shot from sand, the player faces a little more toward the hole.

CRENSHAW:

There are no appreciable differences between the way Bob Jones played bunker shots and the way we play them today.

■ Sand Play

CRENSHAW:

As with his other shots, Bob employed a narrower stance than what is fashionable today. It's amazing just how narrow he stood with any little shot he played.

JONES:

The stance is open with the right foot advanced,…

CRENSHAW:

Although I use a wider stance, I approach sand shots in the same manner.

CRENSHAW:

The sand shot today has become easier than it was in Jones's time for two reasons. First, the sand we now play out of is more uniform. Second, and more important, the modern sand wedge, with the wide flange on the bottom, literally splashes the ball out of the bunker. Note the wide flange on the bottom of today's sand wedge in the inset photo.

JONES:

…and the face of the club is laid off, so that its effective loft is increased.

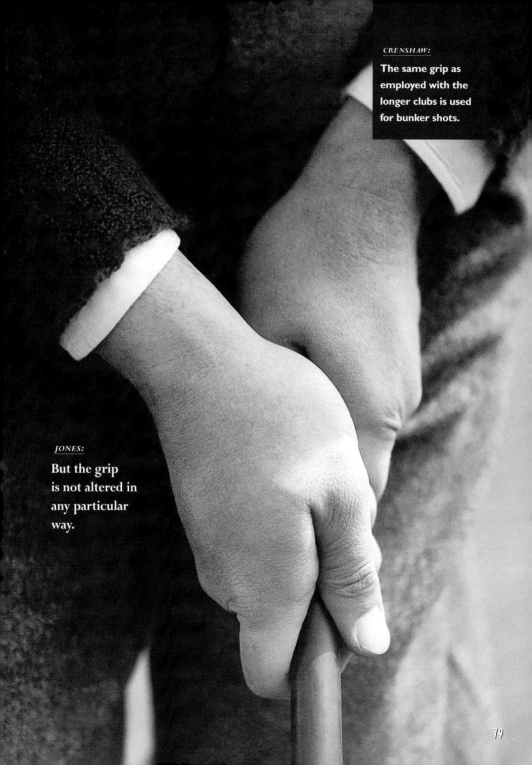

The same grip as employed with the longer clubs is used for bunker shots.

JONES:

But the grip is not altered in any particular way.

79

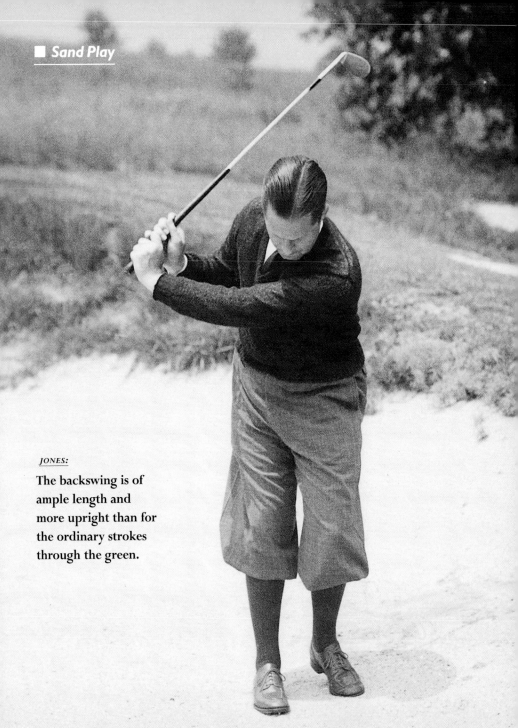

JONES:

The backswing is of
ample length and
more upright than for
the ordinary strokes
through the green.

While Bob tended to
cock his wrists more,
mine is more of an
arm swing.

If you're having
trouble making
contact with a short
shot, try standing
with your feet closer
together. This will
make your feet,
ankles and knees
more active and will
give you a sense of
rhythm and timing.

■ Sand Play

CRENSHAW:

With a sand shot, if you're having trouble making good contact, try experimenting with the position of the ball in the sand.

JONES:

The clubhead cuts across the line of play from outside to inside, or from right to left,…

CRENSHAW:

To play a shot to a pin cut close to the bunker where it's necessary to stop the ball quickly, I widen my stance and bend my knees more. One of the easiest ways to add height to the shot is to feel like you're sitting down on your right knee at address. You might also wish to choke up a little.

You should feel as if you're "under" the ball more and have a wider base.

83

JONES:

...and literally blasts the ball out of the bunker, along with a considerable amount of the sand upon which it is resting.

CRENSHAW:

The finish of this shot makes me think the ball was somewhat buried. Note that the position of his hands and wrists have not changed appreciably from the address position.

When you play a shot out of a buried lie you need to keep your hands moving toward the hole without turning over, just as Bob is demonstrating on the opposite page.

To play this shot, hit down sharply at the edge of the crater formed behind the ball and drive the clubhead down into the sand.

■ Sand Play

JONES:

This is the safest shot to play in order to make certain of getting out of the bunker...

CRENSHAW:

One of the most difficult shots in golf is the long bunker shot. The keys to this shot—whether you're in a green-side bunker or a fairway bunker—are to concentrate on your balance and, especially from a fairway bunker, to take enough club.

With long bunker shots, it is important to contact the sand a little closer to the ball. Since these shots are the converse of the short bunker shot, it is also important to stand a little taller to the ball.

CRENSHAW:

Even though course
maintenance
has improved
dramatically since
Bob Jones's day,
playing a shot from
under a high bank
is still just as difficult.

JONES:

...especially when
the ball is lying
under a high bank.

37

■ Sand Play

CRENSHAW:

This is more of a shot that you'd play off the fairway when you want to roll it a great distance. Play it off your back foot and give it a firm downward rap on the back of the ball.

JONES:

When the ball is resting on firm sand, and the wall of the bunker is not too high, a clean chip may be attempted.

When successful, this little
shot is a great stroke-saver,
but it involves a deal of
risk.

CRENSHAW:

Since it's been more
fashionable to play
most shots in the air
today, rather than
on the ground, this
type of shot is a
fine one to add to
your repertoire and
use under the right
circumstances—
whether you're in the
bunker or on the
fairway.

■ Sand Play

CRENSHAW:

Note how Bob's head is being directed toward the hole as he rotates his body through the shot. It's totally natural.

JONES:

The stroke must be directed downward for if the club strikes the sand before the ball, disaster results, taking first the ball and then the sand,...

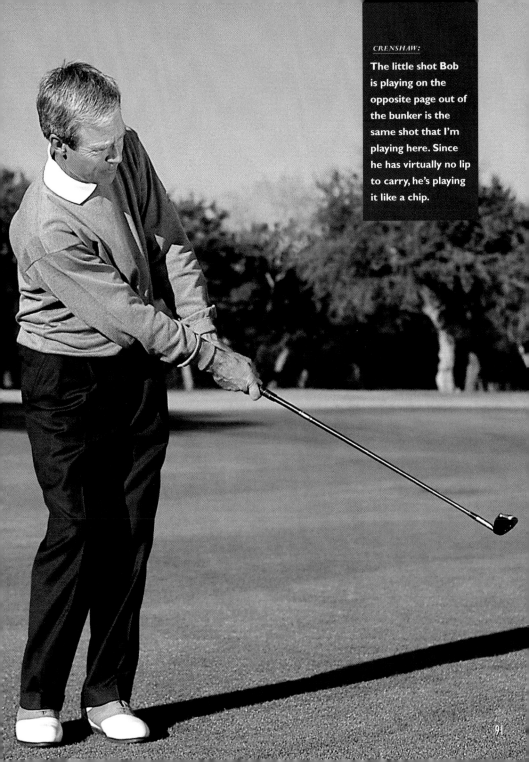

CRENSHAW:

The little shot Bob is playing on the opposite page out of the bunker is the same shot that I'm playing here. Since he has virtually no lip to carry, he's playing it like a chip.

JONES:

...for otherwise the result can be disastrous.

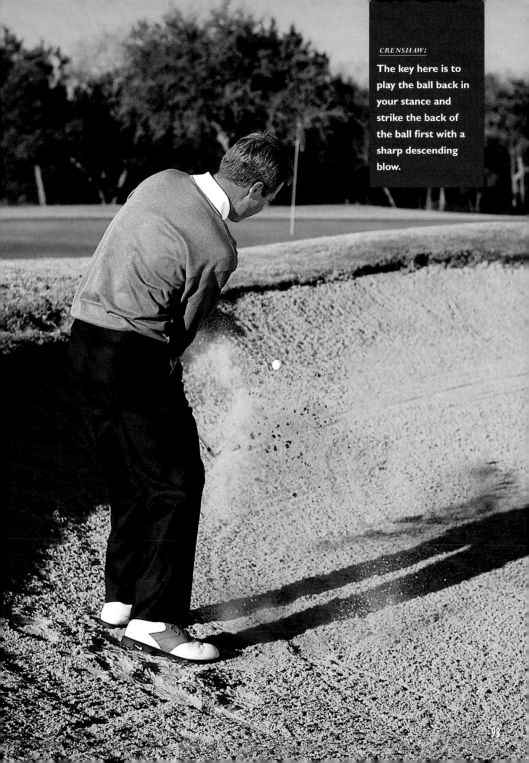

The key here is to play the ball back in your stance and strike the back of the ball first with a sharp descending blow.

Putting

JONES:

In putting, the index finger of the left hand overlaps the little finger of the right instead of the reverse as in the other strokes.

CRENSHAW:

The putting grip Bob employed is the same as is generally used today—palms opposed, thumbs directly down the shaft with the fingers fitting around it as the left index finger fits on top of the space between the little finger and ring finger of the right hand.

95

JONES:

Both thumbs are
along the top
of the shaft so that
the two hands are
directly opposed.

CRENSHAW:

**This putting grip
promotes the wrists
working in unison.**

In gripping the putter, I want it to feel as natural as possible.

I have built my putting grip by using the flat top of the putter handle as a guide. As with Bob's grip, I too place my thumbs directly down the shaft.

I start my putting stroke with a little forward press so that my hands are ahead.

■ **Putting**

JONES:

The posture at address is one of comfort and complete relaxation. The knees are slightly bent to avoid any feeling of tension in the player's underpinning.

CRENSHAW:

Interestingly, Bob's putter, Calamity Jane, featured a round grip and was about 34 inches long. It was a light blade with a slight offset. It was one he thought he could *swing* well.

Importantly, Bob's eyes are not directly over the ball—they are slightly *inside* the ball. This position permits freedom in the putting stroke.

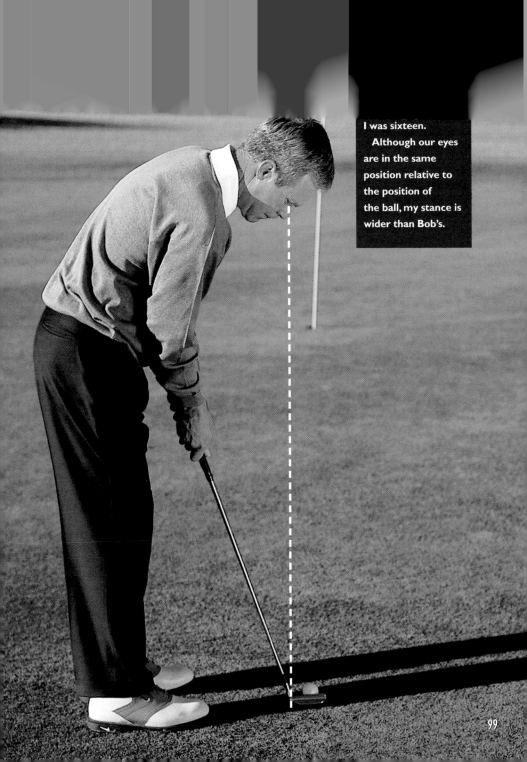

I was sixteen. Although our eyes are in the same position relative to the position of the ball, my stance is wider than Bob's.

■ Putting

JONES:

The feet are close together and the weight about evenly divided between the two. The left elbow is away from the side so that it can move forward without hindrance.

CRENSHAW:

Today, many believe a prerequisite to good putting is to keep your eyes directly over the ball. Notice that his eyes are lined up *behind* the ball.

Note how close his feet are together. No other great player stood with as narrow a stance as Bob Jones.

Also note that his left arm is bent at the elbow. Consequently, his left shoulder is lower than mine at address.

CRENSHAW:

Although my stance is somewhat wider, my head position is further *behind* the ball than Bob's.

My position at address is a little more erect and my left shoulder is higher because the left arm is straighter.

The most important aspect in putting is to be comfortable and relaxed over the ball.

JONES:

No attempt is made
to "hinge" the stroke
upon either the right or
the left wrist. The arms
and shoulders assist
in the action and the
hips and legs yield
to the movement as the
need arises.

CRENSHAW:

By keeping the left
elbow out from his
body, he wants the
putter face, left hand
and left arm to go
back and toward the
hole. He wanted the
clubface to "float"
through the ball.

CRENSHAW:

This picture illustrates several principles of good putting:
- Bob's head has stayed down through the put well after he stroked the ball,
- He's still looking at the same spot as he was at address.

JONES:

To step or lock the left wrist before or as the club strikes the ball is a serious mistake. The left arm must move forward to permit a smooth completion of the stroke.

103

JONES:

The backswing brings the club slightly inside the projected line of the putt and the blade is allowed to open naturally.

CRENSHAW:

I couldn't agree more about the path of the backswing; it needs to come slightly inside the line. This is exactly how I feel taking the putter back.

JONES:

The club continues its swing in a flat arc close to the ground and...

CRENSHAW:

Many instructors now recommend a static or rigid position for the lower body coupled with a one-piece movement of the shoulders and hands back and through.

I strongly disagree with this philosophy because a rigid lower body only adds to tension.

Note how much Bob's lower body, particularly his knees and hips, has moved from the photo on page 104 to this photo and then to the photo on page 108.

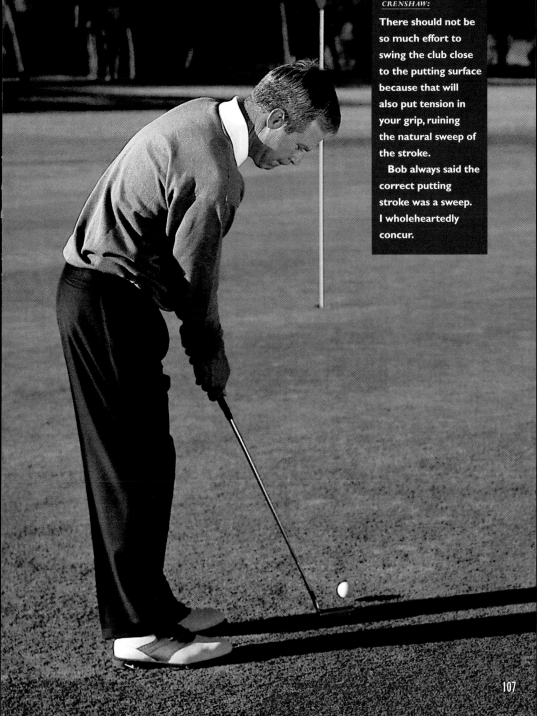

There should not be so much effort to swing the club close to the putting surface because that will also put tension in your grip, ruining the natural sweep of the stroke.

Bob always said the correct putting stroke was a sweep. I wholeheartedly concur.

JONES:

…finishes in a sweep that is not restricted by taut muscles.

CRENSHAW:

Note how this is a very smooth, rhythmical sweep.
  Bob felt that putting was simply the ability to gauge a slope and put the proper pace on the ball.

CRENSHAW:

The feeling of comfort and relaxation without any rigidity at any point in the putting stroke is the ideal.

As Bob Jones said many times, any stroke in golf must be a swing.

■ Putting

CRENSHAW:

It appears that Bob is playing this little chip with a "chipper" that was made for him to produce run-up shots.

There's no difference in the way Bob is addressing the ball than he does with his putter. However, since the club has a little loft, he's playing it back in his stance.

JONES:

The little chip, from just off the green, becomes in reality a putt…

…when played with a special club of the length and lie of a putter,

CRENSHAW:

Harvey taught us to play a little 6- or 7-iron from just off the green to play this shot. He wanted us to feel some movement in our lower body. He emphasized that a putt should feel the same way.

JONES:

...but with enough loft to pitch the ball onto the closely cut putting surface.

CRENSHAW:

This is a great drill to feel the "swing" of a putt. It's basically the same shot.

113

■ *Putting:*
A Comparison

THRU 14

| HOCH | 7 |
| CRENSHAW | 10 |

OR	PAR	4	5	4	3	4	3	4	5
4	ELKINGTON	4	5	5	5	5	6	6	6
4	COUPLES	4	4	5	6	6	5	6	6
8	HOCH	8	8	9	8	7	7	7	7
7	CRENSHAW	7	7	7	8	8	8	8	8
1	STRANGE	2	3	4	4	4	5	4	5
7	FROST	7	7	7	7	7	7	7	7
7	MICKELSON	6	5	5	5	5	4	4	6
6	HENNINGER	6	6	6	7	7	8	7	8
3	NORMAN	3	4	4	4	4	5	5	6
9	HAAS, J.	9	9	7	6	6	5	5	6

■ Chipping

CRENSHAW:

Bob Jones always said never loft the ball unless you absolutely have to. That's still a great piece of advice.

JONES:

Up this close, a number of four or five may be used, and the ball allowed to take its normal roll. The backswing must be of ample length,…

121

JONES:

...so that the club may be swung through smoothly, without jerk or hurry.

CRENSHAW:

What's important in short shots around the green is the concept of a swing. It's not a stab, it's not a push and it's not a lunge.

CRENSHAW:

In chipping, it's
important to simply
let the club swing
back and through.
That effort alone will
make the ball go.

■ Chipping

CRENSHAW:

There's no better way to express any chip shot than to just get the ball on the green and let it role the intervening way to the hole.

JONES:

Back a bit further, since you still want to pitch to the green without spin if possible, you select a more lofted club, say a number eight,…

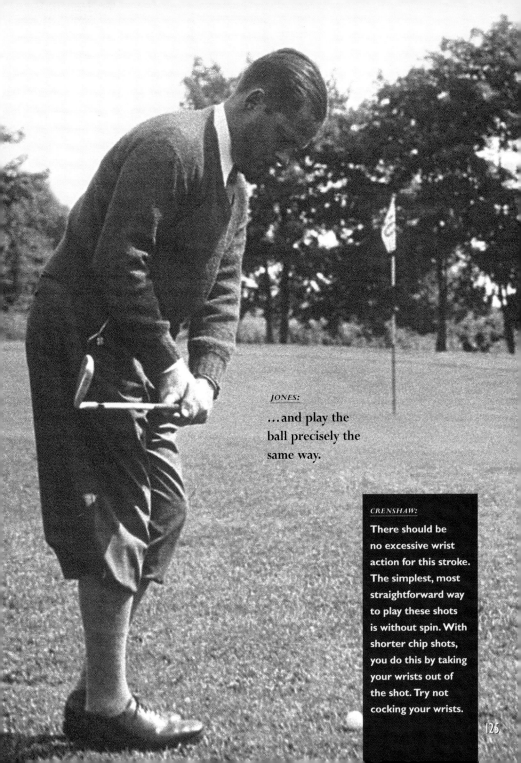

JONES:

…and play the
ball precisely the
same way.

CRENSHAW:

There should be
no excessive wrist
action for this stroke.
The simplest, most
straightforward way
to play these shots
is without spin. With
shorter chip shots,
you do this by taking
your wrists out of
the shot. Try not
cocking your wrists.

125

JONES:

A straightforward pitch, without attempting anything fancy, is always the safest course.

127

JONES:

There is nothing
fundamental which
distinguishes this
stroke from any
other. The initial
position is entirely
comfortable, the feet
are close together
to make the slight
turn of the hips
a bit easier,…

JONES:

...there is ample use of the hands in the backswing,...

JONES:

…and the crisp, decisive stroke at the same time retains its smooth, flowing quality.

CREASTER.
I am simply trusting
the loft of the
clubhead in order
to play this shot.
I can't tell you how
many times Harvey
would tell us "you're
not trusting the
manufacturer to get
the job done." In
other words, let the
clubhead do the work
it was designed for.

JONES:

When you get back this far, or have to pitch over a bunker, you choose a niblick, but again, unless the circumstances are extraordinary, you rely upon a normal shot.

CRENSHAW:
This is a good example of needing to loft the ball to get over a bunker. Simply swing the weight of the club and let the club do the work that it was designed to do.

133

JONES:

The main thing
is to assure a
complete cocking
of the wrists, a
firm left arm, and
a backswing that
is of ample length.

CRENSHAW:

I think any modern
player would do well
to remember that
the concept behind a
short shot is still a
swing.

JONES:

It is better to
have to "float"
the club against
the ball than
to have to make up
for a too-short
backswing by any
extraordinary
effort.

135

JONES:

From a lie like this, a short pitch over a bunker provides one of the most difficult problems in the game. You cannot know precisely how much cushioning effect the grass will have.

JONES:

But if you lay back the face of your niblick and loft the ball high in the air you are not likely to go far astray.

This shot is not any different today, except that there is no need to lay back the face of the club. Our specialty wedges today have plenty of loft to accomplish this type of shot. Obviously, this stroke is as important today as it was yesterday.

The Stymie

CRENSHAW:

The stymie, as a specialty shot in match play, was legislated out of existence in 1952 when the USGA permitted marking a ball on the green that interfered with play.

■ *The Stymie*

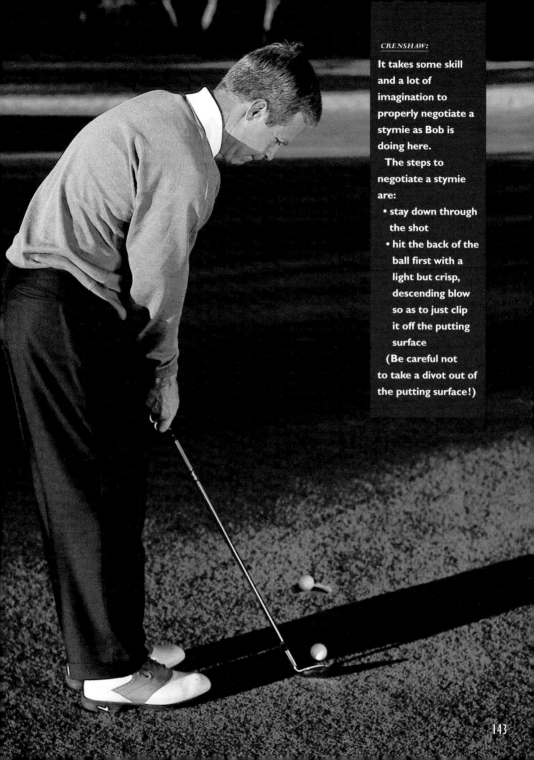

CRENSHAW:

It takes some skill and a lot of imagination to properly negotiate a stymie as Bob is doing here.

The steps to negotiate a stymie are:

- stay down through the shot
- hit the back of the ball first with a light but crisp, descending blow so as to just clip it off the putting surface

(Be careful not to take a divot out of the putting surface!)